A LITTLE BOOK FOR A

Friend

D1785071

HELEN EXLEY ®

A friend's writing
on an envelope
lifts the heart on
the rainiest morning.

CHARLOTTE GRAY

Two people sitting over a pot of tea and hot buttered teacakes push all the huge international anxieties to the edges of perception — and live for a little while in an Eden of their own.

PAMELA DUGDALE

WITHOUT WORDS

Part of what friends
experience is something
that people who aren't
friends can't know.
It's a code.
It's another language.

JUDD NELSON

Shout and everyone hears
what you say.
Whisper and those close
hear what you say.
Be silent and your best
friend hears what you say.

LINDA MACFARLANE

A true friend is someone
who is there for you when they're
supposed to be somewhere else.

LINDA MACFARLANE

Friends are a wonderful excuse
to stop whatever you were doing.

CHARLOTTE GRAY

FUN DAYS!

A friend calls you up
on a sudden summer's day
and says "Drop everything...
we're going out
into the country and finding
ourselves lunch."

PAM BROWN, b.1928

CALL ME!

Friends are there on the end
of the telephone.
When your hopes are ravelled
and your nerves are knotted,
talking about nothing in
particular, you can feel
the tangles untwist.

PAM BROWN, b.1928

When you need to whine about
things going wrong.
When you need to moan about
life's little injustices.
A friend is happy just to listen
to your tales of woe.
And finally when you've moaned
your last moan,
together you can laugh
about it.

LINDA MACFARLANE

Old, old friends on shopping
expeditions have legs that give out
at the same moment – which
means a co-ordinated move to
the nearest cafe.

PAM BROWN, b.1928

BONDS

There are limits
to our friendship –
the sky.

LINDA MACFARLANE

I said "friendship
is the greatest bond in
the world," and I had
reason for it, for it is
all the bands
that this world hath;

JEREMY TAYLOR

RELAXED TOGETHER

What is a friend?

I will tell you.

It is a person with whom

you dare to be yourself.

FRANK CRANE

Friends have the uncanny capability of recognizing the existence of the same, kind, normal you — when the rest of the world is aghast at your unreasonable manner.

CHARLOTTE GRAY, b.1937

IF A TRUE FRIENDSHIP
CAN BE FOUND, CHERISH IT
LIKE A FINE GEM.
POLISH IT, GO OUT OF YOUR WAY
TO KEEP AND PROTECT IT.
KEEP IT SAFE, BUT LET IT SHINE
FOR ITSELF.
IT WILL GROW
AND GROW.

MARY SWANEY

ON YOUR SIDE

Seeing a good friend
is like going home, or like
tasting Mother's cooking.
I feel secure, and need not
protect myself.
"Here," I say, "it is safe,
for I am loved."

ARNOLD R. BEISSER, b.1925

FRIENDS

KNOW EXACTLY WHO YOU

REALLY ARE —

SO YOU DON'T HAVE

TO PRETEND.

CHARLOTTE GRAY,
b.1937

"I'll be right there"
is the best promise
a friend makes.

HELEN THOMSON, b.1943

With a friend at your
side, no road seems
too long.

JAPANESE PROVERB

Being a friend,
I do not covet gold,
or the royal gift
to give him pleasure,
but sit with him
and have him hold
my hand.

AIDS PATIENT

RESPECT

Throughout all eternity –
including now –
the deep respect and trust
of a friend is probably
the most satisfying of life's
experiences.

WALTER MACPEEK

When friends ask,
there is no tomorrow.

PROVERB

To fall down you manage
alone but it takes friendly
hands to get up.

YIDDISH PROVERB

WHAT DO WE LIVE FOR,
IF IT IS NOT TO
MAKE LIFE LESS DIFFICULT
FOR EACH OTHER?

GEORGE ELIOT
(MARY ANN EVANS)
(1819-1880)

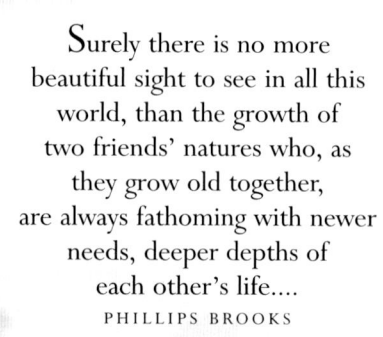

Surely there is no more
beautiful sight to see in all this
world, than the growth of
two friends' natures who, as
they grow old together,
are always fathoming with newer
needs, deeper depths of
each other's life....

PHILLIPS BROOKS

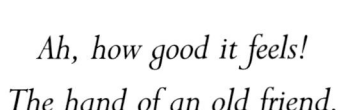

Ah, how good it feels!
The hand of an old friend.

HENRY WADSWORTH
LONGFELLOW (1807-1882)

Other people come and
other people go, and you
do not care; but, when
this person comes,
sunshine comes, the air
is clearer, there is more
life in it, the flowers

grow more beautifully,
the sky is fairer, and the
night is deeper. All the
earth grows glad; and
there is a new note in
the song of the birds.

M. J. SAVAGE

A real friend is one who walks in when the rest of the world walks out.

WALTER WINCHELL

Friendship is a sheltering tree.

SAMUEL TAYLOR COLERIDGE
(1772-1834)

I love you for putting your hand into my heaped-up heart and passing over all the foolish and frivolous and weak things that you can't help dimly seeing there, and for drawing out into the light all the beautiful radiant belongings that no one else had looked quite far enough to find.

ROY CROFT

THE ONLY GOOD TEACHERS
FOR YOU ARE THOSE FRIENDS
WHO LOVE YOU,
WHO THINK YOU ARE INTERESTING
OR VERY IMPORTANT,
OR WONDERFULLY FUNNY.

BRENDA UELAND

FRIENDS
DON'T EXPECT YOU
TO BE PERFECT.
IN FACT —
THEY ARE UTTERLY
ASTONISHED
WHEN YOU ARE.

PAMELA DUGDALE

Every man should
have a fair-sized
cemetery in which to
bury the faults of
his friends.

MARK TWAIN
(1835-1910)

It's always amazing
what a friend can
forgive.

AUTHOR UNKNOWN

UNDERSTANDING

There is nothing we like to see
so much as the gleam of
pleasure in a person's eye when
he feels that we have
sympathized, understood,
interested ourself in his welfare.
At these moments something
fine and spiritual passes

between two friends. These moments are the moments worth living.

DON MARQUIS, FROM "PREFACES"

FRIENDSHIP IS LOVE WITH UNDERSTANDING.

FRANCIS GAY,
FROM "THE FRIENDSHIP BOOK OF
FRANCIS GAY"

A friend is the one person
you like to knock at your door
when you have something spotty
and sniffly and hot.
You may say "Don't come in
for goodness sake."
But you hope she says,
"Nonsense. Get back to bed.
I'll put the kettle on."

PAM BROWN, b.1928

It's just the little homely things,
The unobtrusive, friendly things,
The "Won't-you-let-me-help-you"
things... That make the world
seem bright.

AUTHOR UNKNOWN

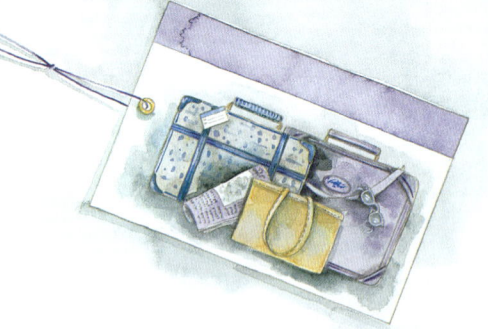

ACROSS THE WORLD

Because of a friend, life is a little
stronger, fuller, more gracious

thing for the friend's existence,
whether she be near or
far. If the friend is close
at hand, that is best; but if she
is far away she still is there to
think of, to wonder about,
to hear from, to write to,
to share life and experience
with, to serve, to honour, to
admire, to love.

ARTHUR CHRISTOPHER BENSON
(1862-1925)

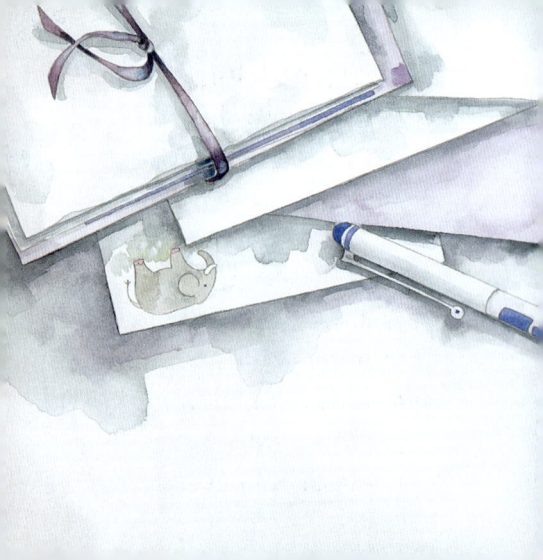

Silences and distances
are woven into the texture
of every true friendship.

ROBERTA ISRAELOFF

Friendship...
does not abolish distance
between human beings
but brings that distance
to life.

WALTER BENJAMIN

Who shall explain
the extraordinary instinct that
tells us, perhaps after a single
meeting, that this or that
particular person in some
mysterious way matters to us?

ARTHUR CHRISTOPHER BENSON
(1862-1925)

I BELIEVE IN FRIENDSHIP
AT FIRST SIGHT.

LINDA MACFARLANE

In MY FRIEND,
I FIND A SECOND SELF.

ISABEL NORTON

A friend notices you getting wistful over something you cannot afford. And gives it to you on your birthday.

CHARLOTTE GRAY,
b.1937

A friend
comes across things
in the market,
two for the price of one.
And she just can't manage
both of them —
so could you use the one
left over?
And, oddly enough,
you can.

PAM BROWN, b.1928

Friends don't give you
flowers or chocolates
for your birthday
or soap or talc or
handkerchiefs.
They bring two sacks
of rotted stable manure
or a brand new hammer.
Friends know what you
actually want.

PAM BROWN, b.1928

OLD FRIENDS

My coat and I live
comfortably together. It has
assumed all my wrinkles,
does not hurt me anywhere,
has moulded itself on my
deformities, and is
complacent to all my

movements, and I only feel its presence because it keeps me warm. Old coats and old friends are the same thing.

VICTOR HUGO (1802–1885)

HORRIBLY HONEST

A very good

friend will tell

you the truth

about your

fruit cake.

PAM BROWN,
b.1928

Only a friend can tell you
your hem is down
or that you've got a smear
of toothpaste on your face
or that you're wearing
odd shoes.

CHARLOTTE GRAY, b.1937

Hearts need friends.

STUART AND
LINDA
MACFARLANE

Friendship is a kindlier loving.

PAM BROWN, b.1928

THE BALM OF LIFE, A KIND AND FAITHFUL FRIEND.

MERCY OTIS WARREN

Kind words of friends can be short and easy to speak, but their echoes are truly endless.

MOTHER TERESA (1910-1997)

We who have friends
are wrapped around in
kindliness
and safe from the cold
immensity of space.

PAM BROWN, b.1928

The best rule
of friendship
is to keep your heart
a little softer than
your head.

GEORGE SANTAYANA
(1863-1952)

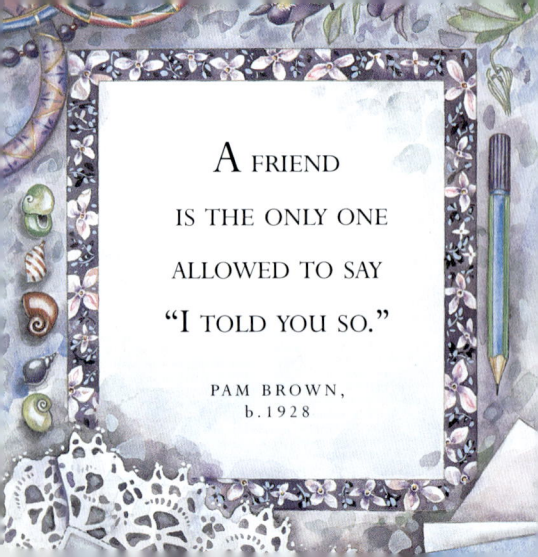

A FRIEND

IS THE ONLY ONE

ALLOWED TO SAY

"I TOLD YOU SO."

PAM BROWN,
b.1928

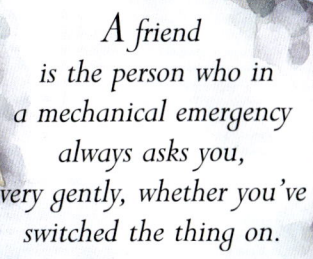

A friend
is the person who in
a mechanical emergency
always asks you,
very gently, whether you've
switched the thing on.

PAM BROWN,
b.1928

BUDDIES

Old friends disintegrate
together — which enlivens
the process.

PAM BROWN, b.1928

What a wretched lot of old
shrivelled creatures we shall be
by-and-by. Never mind —
the uglier we get in the eyes of
others, the lovelier
we shall be
to each other.

GEORGE ELIOT
(MARY ANN EVANS)
(1819-1880)

So long as we love we serve;
so long as we are loved by
others, I would almost say
that we are indispensable;
and no man is useless while
he has a friend.

ROBERT LOUIS STEVENSON
(1850-1894)

The most I can do for my friend

is simply to be his friend.

I have no wealth to bestow

upon him. If he knows

that I am happy in loving him

he will want no other reward.

Is not friendship divine

in this?

LAVATIN

Happiness is made to be shared.

FRENCH PROVERB

Happy is the house that shelters a friend.

RALPH WALDO EMERSON
(1803-1882)

Much of the pleasure in doing
something new comes from the
thought of telling a friend all about it.

LINDA MACFARLANE

The very best thing is good talk, and the thing that helps it most is friendship. How it dissolves the barriers that divide us, and loosens all constraints, and diffuses itself like some fine old cordial through all the veins of life — this feeling that we understand and trust each other, and wish each other heartily well!

HENRY VAN DYKE

Money can buy many things, good and evil. All the wealth of the world could not buy you a friend or pay you for the loss of one.

G.D. PRENTICE

THERE ARE TIMES WHEN I HAVE
NEEDED TO TELL SOMEONE MY
FEAR, TIMES WHEN I HAVE NEEDED
SOMEONE TO SHARE A SECRET,
TIMES WHEN I HAVE NEEDED
SOMEONE TO REJOICE WITH ME
OVER AN ACHIEVEMENT. AND THOSE
ARE THE TIMES WHEN ONLY MY
FRIEND WILL DO.

PAM BROWN, b.1928

I praise the Frenchman,
his remark was shrewd —
How sweet, how passing
sweet, is solitude!
But grant me still a friend
in my retreat
Whom I may whisper —
solitude is sweet!

WILLIAM COWPER

"Stay" is a charming word
in a friend's vocabulary.

AMOS BRONSON ALCOTT

When we can share —
that is poetry in the prose
of life.

SIGMUND FREUD

Yes, there is a talkability that can express itself even without words. There is an exchange of thought and feeling which is happy alike in speech and in silence. It is quietness pervaded with friendship.

HENRY VAN DYKE

THE LITTLE THINGS

The potted plant
on your doorstep
with no message is from
your friend.

PAM BROWN, b.1928

Life is not made up of great sacrifices and duties but of little things: in which smiles and kindness given habitually are what win and preserve the heart and secure comfort.

SIR HUMPHREY DAVY

Away from Loneliness

Those who are unhappy have no need for anything in this world but people capable of giving them attention.

SIMONE WEIL (1909-1943)

Friendship needs no words —
it is solitude delivered from
the anguish of loneliness.

DAG HAMMARSKJOLD (1905-1961)

There is no desire so deep as the
simple desire for companionship.

GRAHAM GREENE (1904-1991)

MY BEST FRIEND
IS THE ONE WHO BRINGS OUT
THE BEST IN ME.

HENRY FORD

Wherever you are it is your own friends who make your world.

WILLIAM JAMES

There is no love so good and so powerful as the one you find expressed in friendship.

SIR LAURENS VAN DER POST

FRIENDS ARE
ALL THAT MATTER.

GELETT
BURGESS

THE GREATEST THING
IN LIFE

Friendship can mean being there, writing a letter or making a telephone call. It can be wispy, ephemeral, solid or pragmatic, last a lifetime or a week. It can leave with bitterness or stay in the memory like a warm, bright gem. Nothing replaces friendship; not money, power, beauty, possessions or fame.

RITA ROBINSON,
FROM "THE FRIENDSHIP BOOK"

FOR A LIFETIME

*To the young, friendship
comes as the glory of the
spring, a very miracle of
beauty, a mystery of birth:
to the old it has the bloom
of autumn, beautiful still.*

HUGH BLACK

We've been friends forever.
I suppose that can't be true.
There must have been a time
before we became friends
but I can't remember it.
You are in my first memory
and all my best memories
ever since.

LINDA MACFARLANE

*What seems to grow fairer to me
as life goes by is the love and
the grace and tenderness of it;
not its wit and cleverness and
grandeur of knowledge — grand
as knowledge is — but just the
laughter of children and the
friendship of friends, and the cozy
talk by the fire, and the sight of
flowers, and the sound of music.*

AUTHOR UNKNOWN